CACTUS FLOWERS

RIO NUEVO PUBLISHERS®
P.O. Box 5250, Tucson, Arizona 85703-0250
(520) 623-9558, www.rionuevo.com

Design: Karen Schober, Seattle, Washington

Front cover: Rainbow cactus, *Echinocereus rigidissimus* • Back cover: Christmas cactus 'Nicol', *Schlumbergera bridgesii* • Page 1: Fishhook pincushion cactus, *Mammillaria grahamii* • Pages 2–3: Santa Rita cactus, *Opuntia santa-rita*

Library of Congress Cataloging-in-Publication Data

Lowell, Susan, 1950-
  Cactus flowers / Susan Lowell.
    p. cm. -- (Look West series)
  ISBN 1-887896-75-9 (hardcover)
  1. Cactus. 2. Cactus--Pictorial works. I. Title. II. Series: Look West
  QK495.C11L76 2005
  583'.56--dc22
                          2004025734

Printed in Hong Kong

10 9 8 7 6 5 4 3 2 1

CACTUS FLOWERS

Susan Lowell

LOOK WEST
SERIES

TUCSON, ARIZONA

HER BEAUTY RADIATES THROUGH THE NIGHT.
AT FIRST IT'S NO MORE THAN A PALE BLUR HOVERING
IN THE DARKNESS. WHEN A FLASHLIGHT CATCHES HER, SHE TAKES
SHAPE AS A STARBURST OF CREAMS AND PINKS, THEN AS AN
OVERSIZE SOFT TEACUP FILLED WITH YELLOW THREADS, AND
FINALLY—AH!—AS A WHIFF OF SOMETHING LUSCIOUS.
SHE CALLS UP MEMORIES OF RIPE MELON, LEMON
BLOSSOMS, COOL WATER, CHANEL NO. 5 ...

Audrey's in bloom. For seventeen years this South American beauty has been a member of our household in Tucson, Arizona. She's grown tall and husky, but she's still a late bloomer. Very late, actually, for Audrey is a night-blooming cereus, and she doesn't really open up till the wee hours of the morning. The best blossoms that we've

Left: Night-blooming cereus, *Cereus peruvianus*
Above: Strawberry hedgehog cactus, *Echinocereus enneacanthus* var. *stramineus,* with lupine

ever seen, a series of gorgeous trumpets six inches long and five across, bloomed during long sleepless nights in June of 1987, when our younger daughter was a newborn night owl. Each of Audrey's flowers lasts only one night.

Not every species blooms with such razzmatazz at night, but all cactus flowers are dramatic: soft, delicate blossoms suddenly spring from a plant that's anything but. The contrast between bristling spines and smooth petals is extreme. "Grotesqueness of form or habit is rarely found in combination with floral beauty in the vegetable world," observed the British Victorian cactologist Lewis Castle, writing in 1884. "No family affords more remarkable examples of this union of widely divergent qualities," he added, "than the great and peculiar Cactus order."

Tony and Suzanne Mace, a renowned pair of contemporary horticulturalists, have this to add: "For those with patience little can compare to the excitement felt when for the first time a cactus plant, which you may have looked after for thirty years, finally produces a magnificent flower."

The phrase "cactus flower" yokes two opposites into a piquant paradox, a mix, perhaps, of pain and pleasure—or, even better, of pain that ends in pleasure. "Cactus blossoms [tell] an enchanted Cinderella story," as Peter Perl said in *Cacti and Succulents*. In the 1960s *Cactus Flower* became the

Porcupine prickly pear, *Opuntia erinacea*

title of a hit Broadway play starring Lauren Bacall, which then became a movie starring Ingrid Bergman. Both aging divas played the title role of a drab and unappreciated middle-aged woman who bursts suddenly into life. "Cactus Flower" is also the name of a scintillating quilt pattern.

Thanks partly to plant breeders but mainly to nature, real cactus flowers are often brilliantly colored, ranging from paper-white to icy green, and from green through many shades of yellow, and from yellow into fiery oranges, deep claret reds, magentas, lipstick- and peppermint-pinks, until they finally fade into the palest of lavenders. The only color missing from the cactus-flower spectrum is blue. However, in central Mexico the cactus *Myrtillocactus geometrizans* is famous for its tasty blue berries, as big as grapes and known as *garambullos*.

Among the flowers of cacti, day bloomers tend to be loudly colorful; night bloomers tend to appear in some more subtle shade of white. Set against the dull greens and grays of the cactus stems, and also against their often vertical lines and solid geometrical shapes, the flowers stand out strongly. They must. Their mission in life is not to delight onlookers but to attract the pollinators that will help transform flower to fruit to seedling to cactus to flower again.

Lady finger cactus, *Echinocereus pentalophus*

However, the peculiar enchantment that lures other species to look, come, touch, smell, and taste may really be that dry-sounding pollination process under another name.

True cactus lovers can be as quirky and obsessive as any other lover. "You have not seen Life," rhapsodized the cactophiles John James Thornber and Frances Bonker, "until you have viewed at least once the wondrous parade of the brilliant cactus flowers, and surveyed the gorgeous painted canvas flung far out over the burning mesas on the Great American Desert." In 1932 these aptly named coauthors produced a curious book on the subject, floridly entitled *The Fantastic Clan: The Cactus Family. Studies of that Unique and Fascinating Growth, the Cactus Plant, Treating of All the Most Important Groups of Cacti Known, with Scientific Accuracy, and Depicting the Charm of the Desert Land, its Magic Spell and Wondrous Lure, in the Great Cactus Area of the World, the American Desert of the Southwest.*

Cactus flowers can stop people in their tracks. At the Arizona-Sonora Desert Museum near Tucson, one of the many outstanding cactus demonstration gardens grows near the museum restaurants. In the spring this garden flames with especially zingy red-orange *Trichocereus* blossoms, drawing such a crowd of admirers

Rainbow cactus, *Echinocereus rigidissimus*

and photographers that traffic jams regularly develop and temporarily block the busy walkway to the food.

Botanists have pointed out relationships between cacti and many other plants, including spinach, roses, violets, passionflowers, and

succulents like ice plant, portulaca, and saltbush. And it is true that cactus flowers sometimes evoke other, totally unrelated blossoms. The frizzy blooms of *Parodia leninghausii* look like yellow carnations. Claret cup prickly pear flowers resemble red poppies. Epiphytic cacti often produce flowers that look like orchids; *Schlumbergera russelliana* produces a dead ringer for a fuchsia; and the Texas species *Echinocereus pentalophus,* also called the ladyfinger cactus, blooms like a wild rose. Sunflower shapes are also common. Many blossoms of the cereus group, including Audrey's, closely resemble lilies, and so do those of the *Matucana,* cold-tolerant Andean cacti from the hedgehog category.

Here in the Sonoran Desert we live in cactus country, and the blooming season runs from March through September, but it peaks in April, May, and June. Every spring, the prickly pears put out yellow flowers shaped like egg cups. Giant saguaros sprout white horns, or possibly crazy heads of curlers, forty feet above the ground. Four otherwise very similar staghorn chollas (*Opuntia versicolor*) may grow side by side, equally raffish and rough, yet each plant may bloom in a different glowing color: amber, chartreuse, dark red, or warm brown. And, utterly blowing their usual cover,

Matucana cactus (Venezuela), *Matucana* sp.

the tiny, drab fishhook cacti produce dainty little pink wreaths reminiscent of hyacinth blossoms.

But Audrey is the only cactus we've ever named. She wasn't christened for exquisitely angular Audrey Hepburn, but rather for Audrey II, the bloodthirsty plant in *Little Shop of Horrors.* "Feed me, Seymour!" the monster cries, speaking out of a big fat bud shaped like our Audrey's. But there the resemblance stops. Totally silent and harmless, our Audrey would never eat a dentist. No, Audrey has become a special pet because of her marvelous flowers, which are more bombastic than any of the native ones—with the exception of the glorious Sonoran Queen of the Night, *la reina de la noche,* also known as Old Lady White Head, whose story is yet to come.

Actually, Audrey is a very typical cactus. Like all of them she's a succulent xerophyte, or a juicy drought-resistant plant. She belongs to a vast plant family comprising between two thousand and three thousand species and ranging from Lilliputian buttons that grow in a thimble to hulking green giants that tower several stories high and weigh many tons. Technically her name is *Cereus peruvianus* (see page 4)—but she sometimes turns up under *Cereus uruguayanus* or *Cereus repandus.* Like all the rest of her cactus relatives, with exceptions that

Beavertail cactus, *Opuntia basilaris*

only prove the rule, Audrey is an American plant, native to the New World.

Botanical names are so controversial and changeable that amateurs may gratefully stand aside from the fray or even retreat to the less exact but often memorable common names. Audrey has two: Peruvian apple cactus and hedge cactus. She even has a monster relative called *Cereus peruvianus monstrosus,* which grows contorted trunks but lovely flowers.

These odd forms, technically called monstrose, crested, or cristate, are rather common among cacti. Sometimes caused by injury, perhaps sometimes by viruses, but probably not by genetic mutations, they occur when the growth points at the tips of stems are disturbed. Occasionally cacti then fan out into undulating patterns; at other times they sprout multiple growth points. Some specimens don't flower normally. However, one remarkable cristate saguaro cactus, reported from Tucson, Arizona, produces flowers and bears fruit not once, as is usual, but twice every year.

Some cactus fruits are as small and dry as peppercorns. Some are as large as plump figs, which they slightly resemble in texture (seedy) and taste (fairly sweet). Many are edible and some are excellent,

Barrel cactus, *Ferocactus* sp.

especially the fruits of some columnar cacti and many prickly pears. "It tasted truly delicious, having the flavor of a lemon with crushed sugar," wrote Lt. William Emory, who sampled prickly pear fruit in the late 1840s as he explored what is now the southwestern boundary of the United States. Other tasters compare the flavor of cactus fruit to strawberry, watermelon, and cucumber, and the versatile prickly pear is a well-established ingredient in Southwestern cuisine. But I have my doubts about *Cereus peruvianus.* Audrey's "Peruvian apples" look like tired pink figs and taste not so much bland as simply moist.

Not surprisingly, the shapes and behavior of cacti have spawned many weird myths and urban legends. Here are a few, all false and some truly fantastic:

1. Cacti never need water.
2. Cacti should be watered a thimbleful at a time.
3. Cacti bloom once every seven years.
4. Cacti can jump.
5. Cacti have poisonous thorns.
6. Cacti will protect you from radiation.
7. Cacti sometimes start ticking and explode, releasing thousands of tarantulas.

Buckhorn cholla, *Cylindropuntia acanthocarpa*

‖ THE CACTUS FAMILY TREE ‖

Botany is a complex and ever-changing science. But for gardening purposes the cactus family can be seen as a central trunk that spreads into several large branches, including the Pereskiae (the leafy cacti), the Opuntiae (the jointed cacti), and the Cacteae (a huge branch with two particularly interesting offshoots, the tree-dwelling Epiphyllanae and Rhipsalidinae).

PERESKIAE: LEAF-BEARERS

Native to tropical forests in the West Indies and South America, these tall, shrubby, slightly succulent plants are the only branch of the cactus family with leaves and stalks. The *Pereskiae* may be the most ancient cacti, and they certainly represent a transitional form between cacti and other green plants.

OPUNTIAE: PRICKLY PEARS AND SPINY SAUSAGES

These are the jointed cacti, which include the large prickly pear clan as well as the bushy, sausage-like chollas. Hardy *Opuntiae,* which have naturalized around the world, grow at altitudes from sea level to 12,000 feet, from Alberta, Canada, all the way south to Tierra del Fuego, and outdoors in 48 of the 50 American states. Sporting either paddle-shaped joints, sausage-like ones, or a sort of intermediate shape, these are the only cacti with tiny spines called glochids.

CACTEAE: CANDLES, HEDGEHOGS, BARRELS, MELONS, AND PINCUSHIONS

This large group comprises about three-fourths of all cactus species, all with funnel-shaped, tubular, stalkless flowers. Audrey belongs to the Candle or Torch subtribe, the columnar *Cereanae.* Like Audrey these cacti grow upright,

with vertical ribs (Audrey has six), and they are often tall and long-lived. Another subgroup embraces, loosely speaking, the Hedgehogs (*Echinocereanae, Echinocactus,* and *Echinopsis*), which are short to medium-sized and heavily armored. The Barrels (*Ferocactus*) are more massive, guarded with fierce hooks and spines. The *Melocactus* or Melon group is relatively short in stature—from six inches to three feet—but strikingly globular in shape. The Pincushions include the *Mammillariae* or Nipple Cacti, a popular group of at least 400 species that are compact, cute, and not very prickly.

EPIPHYTIC CACTEAE: TREE-HUGGERS

There are two main groups of tree-dwelling or epiphytic cacti: the *Epiphyllanae,* often called the orchid cactus, and the *Rhipsalidanae.* Epiphytic cacti include the very decorative and easy-to-grow Christmas cactus (*Schlumbergia,* a hybrid). The *Rhipsalis* or Mistletoe group, mostly Brazilian, likes the same rain forest environment as orchids and bromeliads. A few species of Rhipsalis are the only cacti to have been found, apparently as natives, outside the Americas. Discovered in Sri Lanka, East Africa, and Madagascar, *Rhipsalis* presents a fascinating mystery. Were the sticky seeds carried by birds? Ocean currents? Man? No one knows.

Above: Red barrel cactus (with common phacelia), *Ferocactus* sp.

Audrey's exact place of origin is uncertain, though clearly South American, and since *Cereus peruvianus* is easy to grow it has long been cultivated elsewhere. Linnaeus first described Audrey's species in 1753, but cacti have fascinated the non-American world from the very beginning, ever since Christopher Columbus first presented one (supposedly a Turk's head) to Queen Isabella of Spain on his triumphant return from the New World. By 1648 the Italian Baroque sculptor Bernini was busy carving a marble prickly pear into the Fountain of the Four Rivers, which still decorates Rome's Piazza Navona today.

Painstakingly cultivated in hothouses or conservatories, cacti became a craze in nineteenth-century England, where Victorian gardeners scheduled cactus parties in honor of their night bloomers, complete with toasts to the flowering plants. In the Southwest, the proper beverage for toasting might be Native American saguaro wine—but wine requires fruit, and fruit comes after flowers. Prickly pear lemonade, flavored and colored pink with delicious bottled syrup made from *Opuntia* fruit, might be the best way to drink to Audrey.

The cactus family, like other succulents, has adapted to dry conditions by developing clever ways to store water in leaves, stems, or

Hedgehog cactus, *Echinocereus* sp.

roots. (In Italian they're humorously called *piante grasse*, or fat plants.) Obesity is only one of many strategies for surviving heat and drought, including specialized flower structure and flowering behavior like Audrey's. Using another strategy, the genus *Copiapoa*, native to the Atacama Desert in Chile, survives on fog.

Alone among all other plants, cacti are remarkable for another trait, their areoles. These are unique organs: slightly raised nubs that dot cactus stems in regular patterns and produce new growth, flowers, fruit … and spines. Cacti have sharp or barbed spines, fairly loosely attached. Succulents such as euphorbias have thorns, which are woody and cannot be detached without injuring the plant. A cactus flower may resemble "a rose in disguise," as Rose Houk gracefully put it in *Wild Cactus,* yet there are interesting differences. For both roses and cactus flowers, sharp weapons do deter enemies. But cactus spines are also vestigial leaves—one of the plant's water-conservation techniques. Regular leaves transpire heavily and would quickly dry out a plant in an arid climate, so in all but a few types of cacti they have been thriftily eliminated. Spines serve to shade the plant, like mini-mini-blinds. Spines also insulate cacti against both heat and cold. So does a special pale frizz, called felt, which is common among *Opuntias,* and long spiderwebby strands, called hair or wool, which is peculiar to cacti such as Audrey's cousins, the Mexican Old Man cactus (*Cephalocereus senilis*) and the Old Man of the Andes (several hairy species of *Orocereus*). At the Paris Exposition of 1889, an Old Man cactus

Pincushion cactus, *Mammillaria plumosa*

entranced Parisians, set off a cactus fad, and almost stole the show from the Eiffel Tower, which was built especially for the exposition.

Audrey's sparse, quarter-inch spines are almost harmless. There are species of cactus that bear seven-inch skewers, or even wickeder thick hooks, like the Texas horse crippler cactus. There's an adage among plant people that you either love or hate cactus, and I'm a cactophile, but to say I always love them would be untrue. Nobody who's ever suffered the pain of cactus spines—especially the nearly invisible but infuriating bristles called glochids—can honestly say that. But it's on the spiniest specimens that beautiful flowers seem the greatest miracle, and the flowers themselves are always smooth and glossy to the touch, even though they are quite unpickable, as cactus-loving Edward Abbey growled protectively in *Cactus Country*.

Cactus flowers generally don't have stems. They spring more or less straight from the areoles, and they are usually solitary, meaning they grow singly rather than in clusters. And unlike most other flowers, cactus blossoms show no clear distinction between their sepals (the modified leaves that form the protective, usually green, calyx of a flower) and their petals (the modified leaves that make up the corolla, or flower itself). Instead there's a gradual transformation from sepals

Fishhook pincushion cactus, *Mammillaria grahamii*

to petals: Audrey's blossoms, for example, begin as a reddish-brown color on the outside of each bud, which as it opens reveals gradations from pink to beige to cream to white to the green innermost petals. Like most other cactus flowers, *Cereus peruvianus* blossoms are constructed in a spiral shape fused at the base to form a tube.

Of course Audrey isn't actually a "she." Virtually all cacti—or rather, cactus flowers—are hermaphrodites, possessing both male and female organs, which in a cactus consist of numerous stamens and a pistil, usually capped off with a large, often star-shaped stigma. Each of Audrey's flowers is filled with at least a hundred slender golden stamens, topped with anthers that tremble on long filaments at the slightest touch. The stamens produce clouds of yellow, powdery, slightly sticky pollen. Some cacti, including certain prickly pears, have sensitive stamens. When disturbed by an insect or poked by a curious finger, they bend en masse toward the stigma, and on a hot day this movement may be distinctly visible. So are the jerks with which a night-bloomer's flowers spring open.

Among cactus flowers the blooms of the *Cleistocactus* are especially unusual. This genus, a branch of Audrey's Cereus group, grows at mile-high elevations in Bolivia. Its name comes from the Greek

Engelmann's prickly pear, *Opuntia engelmannii*

word *kleistos,* or closed, and it describes the two-inch, cylindrical crimson or orange flowers—which only barely open. Just the tiny tips of the stamens, style, and stigma peek out from the end of the vivid flower tube.

Frailea, a genus of small South American hedgehogs, takes this behavior a step farther; their flowers often don't open at all. Instead, self-fertilization produces fruit and seeds within the tightly sealed blossom, and occasionally *Frailea* even bypasses the flower stage entirely. Buds simply become fruits. Taking another developmental path, the *Melocacti* put their energy into growing a colorful, hairy headpiece, or cephalium, rather than into flowers. Their small blossoms must then burst through the ball of fuzz, which sets them off strikingly, like candies on a cupcake.

As for texture, some day-blooming cactus petals have a special glittering sheen like metallic paint, perhaps to catch and reflect sunlight. Most cactus flowers are waxy to resist the heat, drought, and wind of arid climates, and night blooming is another strategy for avoiding these dangers. And since flowering itself demands a huge outlay of energy and water, many succulents have developed the ability for an entire population to bloom at once for maximum

Strawberry hedgehog cactus, *Echinocereus enneacanthus* var. *stramineus* pollination efficiency—which sometimes seems to occur with night blooming cerei, such as Audrey. Noticeable colors, shapes, and scents also attract pollinators quickly to do their work.

The combination can be dizzying, but there's no use putting the flower in the refrigerator overnight. It will be a shriveled shadow of its glorious self in the morning. A person can detect the heady scent of our Sonoran Queen of the Night, *Peniocereus greggii,* at least a hundred feet away from the luminous blossom; the Tohono O'odham or Desert People call it the "Ghost Smell." Commercial perfume makers have tried to bottle the fragrance: "Night Blooming Cereus—a nocturnal desert flower that blooms only once a year; truly special … For those who delight in extraordinary!" But once again, it's not the same.

Ask any bat. Night bloomers attract nocturnal pollinators, including birds and moths as well as many species of bats, and cactus flowers and their pollinators have evolved to work together. Colors like yellow and red are particularly attractive to day-pollinators such as bees, butterflies, and hummingbirds. Nutritious, vibrantly colored pollen attracts birds as well as insects and mammals. Some cactus flowers, such as those of our local saguaros, bloom from afternoon to

Honeybee on Texas prickly pear, *Opuntia lindheimeri*

‖ FLOWER POWER ‖

With a flick and a flap, a lesser long-nosed bat (officially *Leptonycteris curasoae yerbabuenae,* but LLNB for short) bellies up to a saguaro cactus blossom and slurps down a sweet drink. How much night-blooming cactus nectar does it take to fuel and fly a bat? When bat biologist Ginny Dalton set out answer to that question, she found herself asking several more:

Bat with saguaro blossom (*Carnegiea gigantea*)

‡ What's the calorie count of a cactus flower?

‡ How many flowers must a bat visit to stay airborne for a night?

‡ How long would that nectar quest take?

She began with the nectar. Saguaro nectar is about 25 percent fruit sugar or fructose. In contrast, honey measures about 42 percent fructose, and classic Coke is approximately 10 percent corn sweetener. Each saguaro flower contains about a milliliter of nectar (around a fourth of a teaspoon), or approximately ten fly-by servings. LLNB stomachs hold .4 ml.

Next she calculated the energy requirements of an LLNB. How much food does a hungry bat need to zip through the night? Judging from research on other bats, she figured that a 1-ounce LLNB burns 20.2 calories per night. An average human being weighing 2,000 ounces, or 125 pounds, needs a 2,000-calorie diet to maintain that weight. "Obviously it takes more energy to operate an ounce of bat than an ounce of human!" Dalton wrote. "Why? Well, for one thing, bats fly—and the energy cost of that is high."

Here comes her batty math:

‡ Calories per milligram of sugar: 4

‡ Milligrams of sugar per microliter (.001 ml) of nectar: 1

‡ Milliliters (1 ml = 1,000 microliters) of nectar per saguaro flower: 1

‡ Total calories in a flower: 960 (nectar is 24 percent sugar)

‡ So how many flowers must an LLNB drain to fuel itself with 20.2 calories? (20,200 divided by 960 = about 21 blossoms)

And how long would that take, allowing 30 seconds per foraging flight? (About 210 visits, or sips, at 30 seconds each, multiplies out to 105 minutes, or 1 hour and 45 minutes of flight and feeding time.)

Data used with permission from Journey North (www.learner.org/jnorth).

early morning and catch a wide variety of pollinators: doves, ants, honeybees, and flickers give way to hawk moths, nighthawks, and lesser long-nosed bats, among others. It's an intricate system that can be disrupted by habitat loss or disease in either plant or animal populations. It's also a system that adapts to change. And we belong to it, too, as we admire and cultivate the animals, the other plants, and the cacti.

At first Audrey was rather short and lived in a pot. That's where she grew on those summer nights seventeen years ago, when we walked the baby and watched an outbreak of forest fires glitter fiercely in the Santa Catalina Mountains twenty miles away. After supper a bud would begin to puff, almost as though some force inside was inflating it; then in ultra-slow motion the petals would start to lift and curl apart, beginning at the tip. Not till after midnight—and much slow pacing with the baby—would the entire blossom reveal itself down to its yellow-green heart, and blow out a huge cloud of perfume.

Now the baby is ready for college. Planted against a high wall in our front yard, Audrey stands twelve feet tall and has branched out. Healthy as she seems, she remains an exotic species here, and her

Claret cup cactus, *Echinocereus triglochidiatus*

blooming behavior is probably different from what it would be at home in South America. Instead of flowering once a year, she's prolific throughout warm weather, blooming off and on from June to October, and she often seems to bud out after a good drink of water, either from the summer rains or a forgotten hose. Unless closely monitored, those buds may come and go unwitnessed by human eyes. Bud today, fruit tomorrow. Audrey is coy, it seems—or sly.

Very early one September morning I walk outside and catch her in the act. Where yesterday there was nothing but a tight green bud, today she flaunts an albino artichoke turned partway inside out. Half open, I estimate. The blossom points directly at the sun. I measure it: about four inches across, five from top to bottom. Fleshy colors smudge the outer tiers of petals and sepals. Inside the big teacup the masses of stamens look almost frosty, like the finest and freshest of corn silk. I catch a lingering scent of honeydew, slightly overripe, a little nasty.

The pollinators are still busy. Gnats hover around the shrinking flower. Several bees are circling, and the most purposeful one dives inside and blunders and tumbles deep into the flower, occasionally walking the stamen filaments as though they were tightropes. The

Giant walking stick on Texas prickly pear, *Opuntia lindheimeri*

bee vanishes; there's nectar at the bottom of the cup. Two more bees cling to inner petals, apparently drunk on nectar or maybe stupefied with pollen, which is scattered everywhere, like rice after a wedding. Cautiously, although the bees seem quite indifferent to me, I put out a finger and touch first one of Audrey's anthers and then the star-shaped, rubbery stigma. The pollen leaves a garish, eggy stain on my skin. As I turn to go in for breakfast, a pair of very small black birds—flycatchers?—whisk up and away from a hackberry tree where they've been perching and watching, sucked in like all the rest of us by Audrey in bloom.

Now I notice a ripe Peruvian apple, an ex-flower, dangling sideways from Audrey's scruffy ribs. Its pink pulp has split open, and I can see a few green, slimy seeds. Inside each one lies a package of biochemistry, tied up tight, or maybe a green giant. What will happen, I wonder, if I plant them?

GROWING CACTI

Cacti need proper light, air, soil, temperature, food, and water. It's important to know if your plant comes from a desert or near-desert habitat, a mountainous area, a grassland or high plateau, or a tropical or subtropical forest. Then you can try to approach its natural climate in your house, greenhouse, or garden.

LIGHT AND AIR

Both are very important. A bright windowsill will often do, but generally cacti will benefit from some time outdoors, if possible. Shield them from sunburn and frost.

SOIL

All cacti need porous, well-drained soil, such as commercial cactus and succulent mix. All-purpose potting soil is not suitable. When

Engelmann's hedgehog, *Echinocereus engelmannii*

potting these plants, protect your hands with gloves, cloth, or newspaper, or grasp plants by a spine-free area. Avoid potting a cactus too deep, and do not overwater a newly potted plant.

TEMPERATURE

Some cacti can tolerate cool temperatures, even down to freezing, especially if they are kept dry. But most are susceptible to hard frost, and too much heat and drought will also kill them.

FOOD

Fertilizer for cacti should be low in nitrogen and used sparingly.

WATER

Cacti need to be watered, not waterlogged. Always let the soil dry out completely between waterings. Epiphytes and semi-epiphytes benefit from misting. In hot, dry weather small plants in small pots may need water several times a week. Bigger ones may wait under cooler conditions for months without harm. In nature almost all cacti spend part of their lives in dormancy, waiting for rain.

Grizzly bear cactus, *Opuntia polyacantha*, with desert mariposa lily, *Calochortus kennedyi*

‖ A FEW EASY BLOOMERS ‖

ASTROPHYTUM "Star cacti," "bishop's cap"; grow outside in full sun with plenty of water in summer; keep cool and dry in winter. Flowers: clear yellow, red, splotched.

Chin cactus, *Gymnocalycium* sp.

CEREUS Fast-growing and husky; may outgrow greenhouses. Flowers: nocturnal, scented, blooming only when plants are mature; white, cream, pink, lilac.

ECHINOPSIS Commonly cultivated, easy to grow indoors. Flowers: often scented, short-lived, white, yellow, carmine, pink.

GYMNOCALYCIUM "Chin cacti"; very easy to grow and flower; give some shade and more water than some. Flowers: scaly buds open to greenish-white, white, pink, carmine, purplish.

HAMATOCACTUS Blooms well in full sunshine. Flowers: mahogany edged with pink; yellow with red.

LOBIVIA High-altitude Andean cacti; easy to grow but need big pots. Flowers: scarlet, brick-red, orange, delicate pink.

MAMMILLARIA Ideal beginners' plants, easy to grow, compact, and quick to bloom. Flowers: small but well-shaped and often plentiful, blooming in rings; pink, red, white.

NOTOCACTI Easy to grow and flower indoors; give full sun and lots of water in summer but keep cool and dry in winter. Flowers: red stigmas are common, with yellow, pink, purple, green, or orange petals.

OPUNTIA Hardy, but because of their sprawling nature, size, and glochids, best grown outdoors. Flowers: red, orange, yellow, green, pink.

PARODIA Give full sun and abundant water in summer, some water in winter. Flowers: red and orange-yellow, yellow shading to orange, fiery scarlet, white.

REBUTIA Very easy to grow, ideal for the novice; give full sun. Flowers: fiery red, bright red, deep salmon pink, dark red, carmine, clear pink, lilac-rose, yellow.

SCHLUMBERGIA "Christmas cactus"; grows like typical houseplant; likes potting soil, frequent misting. Flowers: magenta, scarlet, pink, white.

TRICHOCEREUS Very vigorous; needs good sun and space, possibly outdoors. Flowers: mostly white night-bloomers; also glowing reds and oranges.

❘❘ OLD LADY WHITE HEAD ❘❘

THE LEGEND OF THE NIGHT-BLOOMING CEREUS

This happened long ago.

In those days everything was closer. The Creator, Elder Brother, often visited the Desert People, and the animals and plants of the desert were more like little people. Sometimes you could talk to them, and they could talk to you.

This was true of Old Lady White Head. She was a tiny, brown, skinny, scrawny, scratchy, dry old woman, but she got that nickname because of her hair. It turned white suddenly when her youngest daughter was captured by Yaquis, fierce enemies who came from far in the south to raid the Desert People.

Years went by, and Old Lady White Head missed her daughter very much. At sunset she used to go to a mound of stones marked with symbols from the past and call to her daughter so far away. And the daughter used to hear and answer her from far away in the south. So this way Old Lady White Head knew that her daughter was alive and well and married to a Yaqui.

But then one day the news was bad. Old Lady White Head could tell that her daughter was in trouble and needed help, but

Saguaro, *Carnegiea gigantea*

— 47 —

the words were too faint to understand. The next day there was nothing.

"I must go to Yaqui country," said Old Lady White Head. "My girl needs me."

"No! No!" cried her neighbors. "It's too far. You don't know the way. You don't speak the language. And you're much too old."

Day after day there was nothing. Finally Old Lady White Head went to the mound of stones at sunset, and there was a small black bird with a message. Her daughter was too sick to send it the usual way, so she had sent the bird to ask her mother to come to her as quickly as she could. The black bird was slow because it had stopped to chatter with other birds in every green spot along the way.

Without telling anyone, Old Lady White Head set off at dawn. The birds woke up and laughed to see such little scrawny brown old lady hobbling along, with her white hair blowing in the wind like dry grass.

"Hey, old lady, let us make a nest on your head!" they called.

"Hey, little people, help yourselves," she answered, and she laughed too.

Wave cactus (also brain cactus), *Stenocactus* sp.

It was a very, very long way to Yaqui country, and Old Lady White Head grew very tired and hungry, but the little bee people fed her honey. When she was lost she asked the way from butterflies, jackrabbits, and coyotes, and they helped her too. When she reached the land of the Yaquis she could not speak their language, but a hawk and a tiny blackbird guided her to the place where her daughter lay with a newborn son in her arms.

"I can't escape," said the daughter, who was dying. "But please save my baby from the Yaquis."

Full of grief and fear, poor Old Lady White Head took the baby and started on her long journey home. But it was dark, and her tearful eyes could not see the stars, so she called for help from the little people all around. First out of the trees came a wolf, who howled, and her little grandson cried because he had never heard that language before.

"Hush," said Old Lady White Head to the baby and the wolf. "Can you help us find our way home to the Desert People?" she asked, but the wolf didn't know the way.

Then an old dry coyote came loping along.

"Ha!" he yelled at the wolf. "You call yourself a wolf? You smell like a skunk and act like a snake. Why are you trying to scare your

Christmas cactus 'Nicol', *Schlumbergera bridgesii*

own people?" Then he turned to Old Lady White Head and said: "I know the way to the desert, and I'll show you."

So off they went, resting during the day and traveling at night. They came out of the mountains and reached the edge of the desert, and the old lady's heart was glad because she thought she was nearly home.

But the coyote shook his head. "I smell Yaquis," he said. "They must be chasing you!"

Old Lady White Head sank down on the ground and cradled her grandson in her skinny, rough brown arms. She knew that she needed more help. So deep, deep inside she began to call out to the desert, to all the people of the desert, both little and big, and to Elder Brother, their Creator.

And Elder Brother answered her call. She must travel by day, he told her, and she must follow the dry riverbeds, or sand washes, and she must never stop till she reached the land of the Desert People in safety. Then she would be happy.

The baby was heavy and the way was long, hot, and hard. But the coyote found the washes for her, and flocks of little black birds warned her when bands of Yaquis came near, hunting her. Then the

Teddy bear cholla, *Cylindropuntia bigelovii*

grandmother would sink onto the sand and sit as still as a rock till they passed by.

Sometimes Elder Brother seemed to walk along ahead of her like a little old man. "Do not be afraid," he said. "You will reach your home and be happy always."

On, on, on they traveled through the washes. Old Lady White Head grew weaker and weaker, until one day when they were nearly home she suddenly heard Yaquis very close. She raised her white head just a little, but they saw her and began to run toward her.

"Elder Brother!" she cried. And far off in the distance she heard him singing the earth song.

Then Old Lady White Head saw the sandy riverbanks come closer and closer, like a landslide. She lifted up her grandson in her arms, and a flock of little black birds came swooping down in a whirling, diving black cloud. Some of the birds attacked the Yaquis while the rest carried the baby safely away.

When the birds released them and disappeared, the Yaquis searched for the old woman, but all they found were some skinny brown sticks and two or three white hairs. Under the sandy earth Old Lady White Head felt cool and safe at last, and she fell asleep.

Prickly pear, *Opuntia* sp.

At sunset Elder Brother came to waken her with good news. Her baby grandson was also safely home in his mother's and grandmother's village.

"I am so happy!" said Old Lady White Head. "But I am still tired. May I rest here always? But there's just one thing—." The old lady hesitated, and then she said: "I'd like to be beautiful."

Elder Brother laughed, and he told her that because she was so brave and kind, so loving and faithful, he would make her wish come true. Like the spindly cereus cactus, with arms like dry sticks and a few straggly white hairs, she could rest underground throughout the year, except for one night each summer. That night Old Lady White Head would become the most beautiful thing in the whole desert world.

And so she is.

(This retelling was inspired by a Tohono O'odham tale collected near Tucson, Arizona, around 1920 by Katherine Kitt and Harold Bell Wright. Another version may be found in Wright's Long Ago Told, *published in 1929.)*

Borzicactus samaipatanus

‖ UNCOMMON NAMES ‖

What's in a name? Of all the plants on Earth, cacti may have inspired the oddest, most descriptive, and most entertaining common names. Would a cactus blossom by any other name smell quite so sweet?

Powder puff	Galloping	Gear stem
Rainbow	Nipple	Sand dollar
Torch	Dancing bones	Button
Indian fig	Rickrack	Organ pipe
Brain	Clock face	Corncob
Feather	Beehive	Eagle claw
Mother-in-law's chair	Turk's head	Fish hook
Goat horn	Old lady	Horse crippler
Dumpling	Angel's wings	Bishop's cap
Living rock	Moon	Pima pineapple
Grizzly bear	Peanut	Beavertail
Compass	Rat tail	Lace
		Dry whiskey

Left: Beavertail cactus, *Opuntia basilaris*
Above: Organ pipe cactus, *Stenocereus thurberi*

‖ WHERE YOU CAN SEE CACTI ‖
IN PUBLIC GARDENS

Arizona-Sonora Desert Museum, Tucson, AZ

Arizona Cactus and Succulent Research, Bisbee, AZ

Balboa Park Old Cactus Garden and Desert Garden, San Diego, CA

Boyce Thompson Arboretum, Superior, AZ

Brooklyn Botanic Garden, Brooklyn, NY

Cacti Mundo Los Cabos Botanical Garden, Baja California, Mexico

Chicago Botanic Garden, Chicago, IL

Chihuahuan Desert Gardens, UTEP, El Paso, TX

Chihuahuan Desert Research Institute, Ft. Davis, TX

Desert Botanical Garden, Phoenix, AZ

Desert Demonstration Gardens, Las Vegas, NV

Ethel M Botanical Cactus Garden, Henderson, NV

The Huntington Botanical Gardens, San Marino, CA

The Living Desert Zoo and Gardens, Palm Desert, CA

Los Angeles County Arboretum & Botanic Garden, Arcadia, CA

Lotusland, Santa Barbara, CA

Mitchell Park Horticultural Conservatory, Milwaukee, WI

Moorten Botanical Garden, Palm Springs, CA

Tree cholla, *Cylindropuntia imbricata*

Quail Botanical Gardens, Encinitas, CA
Rio Grande Botanical Gardens, Albuquerque, NM
San Antonio Botanical Garden, San Antonio, TX
Tohono Chul Park, Tucson, Arizona
Tucson Botanical Gardens, Tucson, AZ
University of California Botanical Garden, Berkeley, CA
UNLV Arboretum, Las Vega, NV
Vermont Experimental Cold-Hardy Cactus Garden, Middlebury, VT

IN THE WILD

Anza-Borrego Desert State Park, Borrego Springs, CA
Big Bend National Park, TX
Living Desert Zoo & Gardens State Park, Carlsbad, NM
Montezuma Castle National Monument, Camp Verde, AZ
Organ Pipe Cactus National Monument, Ajo, AZ
Sabino Canyon Recreation Area, Tucson, AZ
Saguaro National Park, Tucson, AZ

Rainbow cactus, *Echinocereus pectinatus*

‖ SUGGESTED READING ‖

Benson, Lyman. *The Cacti of the United States and Canada.* Stanford, CA: Stanford University Press, 1982.

Humphreys, Anna, and Susan Lowell. *Saguaro: The Desert Giant.* Tucson, AZ: Rio Nuevo Publishers, 2002.

Mace, Tony, and Suzanne Mace. *Cactus and Succulents: A Care Manual.* San Diego, CA: Laurel Glen Publishing, 2001.

Pizzetti, Mariella. *Simon & Schuster's Guide to Cacti and Succulents.* Ed. Stanley Schuler. Trans. Cynthia Munro. New York: Simon & Schuster, 1985.

Quinn, Meg. *Cacti of the Desert Southwest.* Tucson, AZ: Rio Nuevo Publishers, 2002.

‖ PHOTOGRAPHY © AS FOLLOWS: ‖